A Potty for Me!

A Lift-the-Flap Instruction Manual

by Karen Katz

LITTLE SIMON

New York London Toronto Sydney

Mommy got
me something.
Whatever
could it be?

A brand new
little potty,
and it's just
for me!

I've always gone in diapers. That's what they are for.

But Mom says
when I'm ready,
I won't need
them anymore.

I try my brand new potty. It kind of feels okay.

But I'm not
ready yet.
I want to
go and play.

Now I've got
a feeling,
and I think that
I could pee.

Mommy takes
my diaper off.
But this potty's
not for me!

Later, when I
go outside
to run and skip
and play—Uh-oh!

I peed in my pants . . .
but Mom says,
"That's okay!"

Then it's time
to snuggle in
and turn off
one last light.

I wear a diaper
while I sleep
so I'll stay dry
all night.

Wake up! Wake up!
Good morning!
I'll try my potty again.

Me and bunny
sit awhile,
but I still don't
think I can!

Later, Mommy
sits with me.
We sit right
there together.

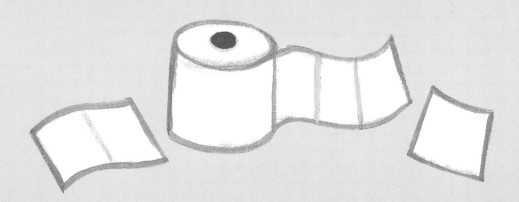

She shows me how
to flush the toilet
and—*whoosh!*—
down goes the water.

Now it's time
to take my bath.
Ooh-hoo!
The water feels so wet.

It makes me feel
like I could go.
Am I
ready yet?

I sit again on
my new potty.
I sit and wait
and sit.

Oh, I hear something in the potty. This time it could be it!

Yeah! I really did it!
And now I
know I can.
I can go in my potty,
and I will do
it again!

No more diapers
now—I'm as happy
as can be.
I get to wear
big kid pants!